CW00996423

365 Days of the Bible: Inspirational Quotes for Christians

Foreword by
M.G. Keefe

365 Days of the Bible:

Inspirational Quotes for Christians

Hot Tropica Books Publication

January 2013

Copyright © 2013 Foreword by M.G. Keefe

Cover illustration copyright © Jackson Falls

ISBN 10: 1481858033
ISBN 13: 978-1481858038

Published by: **Hot Tropica Books**

Synopsis

This massive collection of quotes was handpicked to encourage people in their daily journey. Each saying or proverb is designed to strengthen and renew the reader's faith in God. Some of the quotes are from people about the Bible and the strength we get or need from the book, and not directly from the Bible.

One of the best things we can do for ourselves is to meditate and read God's word regularly. If you are looking for inspiration, check out 365 Days of the Bible. You can sit and read the entire book in one sitting or start off every day with an inspirational verse.

"Whosoever trusteth in the Lord, happy is he." ~ Proverbs 16:20

Foreword by MG Keefe

The Bible is a gift from God and keeping his word close to our hearts helps us to live a better Christian life and love those around us.

There are many famous Bible quotes, but this collection was gathered together to inspire and motivate us to follow God's light and keep us on the right path. If you are looking for a direction in life or to maintain your focus in staying on the righteous path and loving others unconditionally, this collection of inspirational and motivational quotes is for you.

It is difficult to limit the choices, when the entire Bible is full of great information, history and wisdom of the ages. Trying to limit this book to the most popular or the most helpful excerpts was not only difficult but nearly impossible. I mean, the entire Bible is there for a reason right? Some people are bound to disagree with my collection, but these are the quotes that touched me personally and I hope will also move you as well.

365 Days of the Bible

Day 1: With God all things are possible. ~ Mathew 19:26

Day 2: May the Lord continually bless you with heaven's blessings as well as with human joys. ~ Psalmss 128:5

Day 3: I can do all things through him who strengthens me. ~ Philippians 4:13

Day 4: Seek ye first his kingdom and righteousness and all these things will be added unto you. ~ Mathew 6:33

Day 5: Blessed are the pure in heart, for they shall see God. ~ Mathew 5:8

Day 6: I will never fail or forsake you. ~ Hebrews 13:5

Day 7: Trust in the Lord with all your heart, and lean not on your own understanding. In all your ways acknowledge Him and He shall direct your paths. ~ Proverbs3:5,6

Day 8: And be kind to one another, tenderhearted, forgiving of one another. ~ Ephesians 4:32

Day 9: God is with you in all that you do. ~ Genesis 21:22

Day 10: It is more blessed to give than to receive. ~ Acts 20:35

Day 11: We love Him, because He first loved us. ~ 1 John 4:9-10

Day 12: For whatever was written was given to us for our learning, that through patience and comfort of the scriptures we might have hope. ~ Romans 15:4

Day 13: Your word is a lamp to my feet, and a light to my path. ~ Psalms 119:105

Day 14: God is our refuge and strength, a very present help in trouble. ~ Psalms 46:1

Day 15: If we confess our sins, He is faithful and just to forgive us our sins, and to cleanse us from all unrighteousness. ~ 1 John 1:9

Day 16: Come to Me, all you who are weary and weighed down with heavy burdens, and I will give you rest. Take My yoke upon you and learn from Me; for I am gentle and humble in spirit. Indeed you will surely find rest in Me. My yoke is easy and My burden is light. ~ Mathew 11:28-30

Day 17: Those who sow in tears will reap a harvest of joy; for though they may weep when going forth to plant their seed, if they persevere, they will undoubtedly return rejoicing—bringing their sheaves with them. ~ Psalmss 126:5-6

Day 18: I will not leave you as orphans; I will come to you. ~ John 14:18

Day 19: Husbands, love your wives, even as Christ also loved the church, and gave himself for it. ~ Ephesians 5:25

Day 20: Without faith, it is impossible to please God. For he who comes to God must believe He exists, and rewards those who diligently seek Him. ~ Hebrews 11:16

Day 21: And be kind to one another, tender-hearted, forgiving one another, even as God for Christ's sake has forgiven you. ~ Ephesians 4:32

Day 22: Know ye that the Lord He is God: it is He that hath made us, and not we ourselves; we are his people, and the sheep of the pasture. ~ Psalmss 100:3

Day 23: It is not good that man should be alone. ~ Genesis 2:18

Day 24: Thou shalt have no other gods before me. ~ Exodus 20:3

Day 25: Thou shalt not avenge, nor bear any grudge against the children of thy people, but thou shalt love thy neighbor as thyself. ~ Leviticus 19:18

Day 26: It is impossible to rightly govern a nation without God and the Bible. ~ George Washington

Day 27: Jesus answered and said unto her, Whosoever drinketh this water shall thirst again: But whosoever drinketh of the water that I shall give him shall never thirst; but the water that I shall give him shall be in him a well of water springing up into everlasting life. ~ John 4:13-14

Day 28: The thief cometh not, but for to steal, and to kill, and to destroy: I am come that they might have life, and that they might have it more abundantly. I am the good shepherd: the good shepherd giveth his life for his sheep. ~ John 10:10-11

Day 29: Honor thy father and thy mother: that thy days may be long upon the land which the Lord God giveth thee. ~ Exodus 20:12

Day 30: So then, faith comes by hearing, and hearing by the word of God. ~ Romans 10:17

Day 31: Jesus saith unto him, I am the way, the truth, and the life: no man cometh unto the Father, but by me. ~ John 14:16

Day 32: A thorough knowledge of the Bible is worth more than a college education. ~ Theodore Roosevelt

Day 33: Love suffers long, and is kind; love does not envy; love does not promote itself, is not puffed up, does not behave badly, seeks not her own, is not easily provoked, thinks no evil; does not rejoice in iniquity, but rejoices in the truth; bears all things, believes all things, hopes all things, endures all things. Love never fails. ~ 1 Corinthians 13: 4-8

Day 34: Therefore, if any man is in Christ, he is a new creation. Old things have passed away; look, new things have come! 2 Corinthians 5:17

Day 35: Cast your burden on Yahweh, and He will sustain you. He will never permit the righteous to be moved. ~ Psalms 55:22

Day 36: Yahweh is good, a stronghold in the day of trouble: He knows who take refuge in Him. ~ Nahum 1:7

Day 37: Yahweh is close to all who call on him—to all who call on him in truth. He will fulfill the desire of those who fear Him; He will hear their cry and save them. ~ Psalms 145:18-19

Day 38: And this is our confidence, that if we pray according to His will, He will hear us, and give us what we ask for, because our desires are in agreement with His thoughts for us. ~ 1 John 5:14-15

Day 39: For the word of God is living and powerful! It is sharper than any two-edged sword, piercing to the dividing of soul and spirit, and of the joints and marrow, and is a discerner of thoughts and intentions of the heart. ~ Hebrews 4:12

Day 40: If you can believe, all things are possible to him who beleiveth. ~ Mark 9:23

Day 41: For the people who dwell at Zion at Jerusalem; you will weep no more, for Yahweh will be gracious to you; He will hear the voices of your cry and answer you. ~ Isaiah 30:19

Day 42: Ask, and it will be given to you. Seek, and you will find. Knock, and the door will be opened to you. For everyone who asks, receives; and he who seeks, finds; and to he whom knocks the door will be opened. ~ Mathew 7:7-8

Day 43: All scripture is given by inspiration of God, and is profitable for teaching, reproof, correction, and instruction in righteousness, that the man of God may be perfect, thoroughly equipped to perform every good work. ~ 2 Timothy 3:16-17

Day 44: Thou shalt love thy neighbor as thyself. ~ Leviticus 19:18

Day 45: O, give thanks unto the Lord, for He is good. ~ I Corinthians 16:34

Day 46: Fear thou not, I will help thee. ~ Isaiah 41:10

Day 47: Wisdom is a fountain of life to him who has it. ~ Proverbs 16:22

Day 48: The Lord will guide you always, he will satisfy your needs in a sun-scorched land. You will be like a spring whose waters never fail. ~ Isaiah 58:11

Day 49: You, O Lord, keep my lamp burning; my God turns my darkness into light. ~ Psalmss 18:28

Day 50: The Lord is good. His love endures forever, his faithfulness endures through all generations. ~ Psalmss 100:5

Day 51: Follow the way of love. ~ I Corinthians 14:1

Day 52: Within the covers of the Bible are the answers for all the problems people face. ~ Ronald Reagan

Day 53: Whosoever trusteth in the Lord, happy is he. ~ Proverbs 16:20

Day 54: Therefore go and make disciples of all nations, baptizing them in the name of the Father and of the Son and of the Holy Spirit. ~ Mathew 28:19

Day 55: For it is by grace you have been saved, through faith—and this is not from yourselves, it is the gift of God. ~ Ephesians 2:8

Day 56: In the beginnings God created the heavens and the earth. ~ Genesis 1:1

Day 57: For all have sinned and fall short of the glory of God. ~ Romans 3:23

Day 58: But you will receive power when the Holy Spirit comes on you; and you will be my witnesses in Jerusalem, and in all Judea and Samaria, and to the ends of the earth. ~ Acts 1:8

Day 59: All scripture is God breathed and useful for teaching, rebuking, and teaching righteousness. ~ 2 Timothy 3:16

Day 60: For the wages of sin is death, but the gift of God is eternal life in Jesus Christ our Lord. ~ Romans 6:23

Day 61: If you believe in your heart, "Jesus is Lord," and believe in your heart that God raised him from the dead, you will be saved. ~ Romans 10:9

Day 62: Therefore, I urge you, brothers and sisters, in view of God's mercy, to offer your bodies as a living sacrifice, holy and pleasing to God—this is true worship. ~ Romans 12:1

Day 63: But God demonstrates his own love for us in this: While we were still sinners, Christ died for us.~ Romans 5:8

Day 64: Then Jesus came to them and said, "All authority in heaven and on earth has been given to me." ~ Mathew 28:18

Day 65: He said to them, "Go into the world and preach the gospel to all creation." ~ Mark 16:15

Day 66: The Word became flesh and made his dwelling among us. We have seen his glory, the glory of his one and only Son, who came from the Father, full of grace and truth. ~ John 1:14

Day 67: Salvation is found by no one else, for there is no other name given under heaven by which we must be saved. ~ Acts 4:12

Day 68: They devoted themselves to the apostles' teaching and to fellowship, to the breaking of bread, and prayer. ~ Acts 2:42

Day 69: "For I know the plans I have for you," declares the Lord, "plans to prosper you and not to harm you, plans to give you hope and a new future." ~Jeremiah 29:11

Day 70: Trust in the Lord with all your heart and lean not on your own understanding. ~ Proverbs 3:5

Day 71: But the fruit of the Spirit is love, joy, peace, patience, kindness, goodness, faithfulness. ~ Galatians 5:22

Day 72: He saved us, not because of righteous things we had done, but because of his mercy. He saved us through the washing of rebirth and renewal through the Holy Spirit. ~ Titus 3:5

Day 73: Do not conform to the pattern of this world, but be transformed by the renewing of your mind. Then you will be able to test and approved what God's will is—his good pleasing and perfect will. ~ Romans 12:2

Day 74: Do not let your hearts be troubled. Trust in God, trust also in me. ~John 14:1

Day 75: I am not ashamed of the gospel, because it is the power of God that brings salvation to everyone who believes: first to the Jew, then to the Gentile. ~ Romans 1:16

Day 76: Therefore, since we have been justified through faith, we have peace through our God, through our Lord Jesus Christ. ~ Romans 5:1

Day 77: Therefore, just as sin entered the world through one man, and death through sin, and in this way death came to all people, because all sinned. ~ Romans 5:12

Day 78: If we confess our sins, he is faithful and just and will forgive our sins and purify us from all unrighteousness. ~ 1 John 1:9

Day 79: If you love me, keep my commands. ~ John 14:15

Day 80: Do your best to present yourself to God as approved, a worker who does not need to be ashamed and who correctly handles the word of truth. ~2 Timothy 2:15

Day 81: Then you will know the truth and the truth will set you free. ~ John 8:32

Day 82: For to us, a child is born, to us a son is given and the government will be on his shoulders. And he will be called Wonderful Counselor, Mighty God, Everlasting Father, Prince of Peace. ~ Isaiah 9:6

Day 83: For everyone who calls on the name of the Lord will be saved. ~ Romans 10:13

Day 84: Therefore, there is now no condemnation for those who are in Jesus Christ. ~ Romans 8:1

Day 85: A new command I give you: Love one another. As I have loved you, so you must love one another. ~ John 13:34

Day 86: And I will ask the Father, and he will give you another advocate to help you and be with you forever. ~ John 14:16

Day 87: Therefore confess your sins to each other and pray for each other so that you may be healed. The prayer of the righteous person is powerful and effective. ~ James 5:16

Day 89: Therefore the Lord himself will give you a sign: The virgin will conceive and give birth to a son, and will call him Immanuel. ~Isaiah 7:14

Day 90: He came as a witness to testify concerning that light, so that through him all might believe. ~ John 1:7

Day 91: I've read the last page of the bible. It's all going to turn out all right. ~ Billy Graham

Day 92: Do not be anxious about anything, but in every situation, by prayer and petition, with thanksgiving, present your requests to God. ~ Philippians 4:6

Day 93: In your relationships with one another, have the same attitude of mind that Jesus Christ had. ~ Philippians 2:5

Day 94: The next day John saw Jesus coming toward him and said, "Look, the Lamb of God, who takes away the sin of the world!" ~ John 1:29

Day 95: The wrath of God is being revealed from heaven against all the godlessness and wickedness of human beings who suppress the truth by their wickedness. ~ Romans 1:18

Day 96: Therefore, since we are surrounded by such a great cloud of witnesses, let us throw off everything that hinders and the sin that so easily entangles. And let us run with perseverance the race marked out for us. ~ Hebrews 12:1

Day 97: Through Him all things were made; without Him nothing was made that has been made. ~ John 1:3

Day 98: And I tell you that you are Peter, and on this rock I will build my church, and the gates of death will not overcome it. ~ Mathew 16:18

Day 99: I have been crucified with Christ and I no longer live, but Christ lives in me. The life I now live in the body, I live by faith in the Son of God, who loved me and gave his life for me. ~ Galatians 2:20

Day 100: Why don't you start believing that no matter what you have or haven't done, your best days are still out in front of you? ~ Joel Osteen

Day 101: I can do all this through Him who gives me strength. ~Philippians 4:13

Day 102: God is spirit, and his worshippers must worship in the Spirit and in truth. ~ John 4:24

Day 103: In the Bible it says they asked Jesus how many times you should forgive, and he said 70 times 7. Well, I want you all to know I am keeping a chart. ~ Hilary Clinton

Day 104: Be sure of this: the wicked will not go unpunished, but those who are righteous will go free. ~ Proverbs 11:21

Day 105: If we ever forget that we are one nation under God, then we will be a nation gone under. ~ Ronald Reagan

Day 106: God always gives his best to those who leave the choice with him. ~ Jim Elliot

Day 107: But whoever listens to me will live in safety and be at ease, without fear of harm. ~ Proverbs 1:33

Day 108: Throughout life people will make you mad, disrespect you and treat you bad. Let God deal with the things they do, cause hate in your heart will consume you. ~ Will Smith

Day 109: You believe that there is one God. Good! Even the demons believe that—and shudder. ~ James 2:19

Day 110: An honest answer is like a kiss on the lips. ~ Proverbs 24:26

Day 111: Be true to yourself, help others, make each day your masterpiece, make friendship a fine art, drink deeply from good books—especially the Bible, build a shelter against a rainy day, give thanks for your blessings and pray for guidance everyday. ~ John Wooden

Day 112: When I stand before God at the end of my life, I would hope that I would not have a single bit of talent left, and I could say, 'I used everything you gave me.' ~ Erma Bombeck

Day 113: There must be a reason why some people can afford to live well. They must have worked for it. I only feel angry when I see waste. When I see people throwing away things that we could use. ~ Mother Teresa

Day 114: The wages of the righteous is life, but the earnings of the wicked are sin and death. ~ Proverbs 10:16

Day 115: God grant me the serenity to accept the things I cannot change, the courage to change the things I can, and the wisdom to know the difference. ~ Reinhold Niebuhr

Day 116: Many people mistake our work for our vocation. Our vocation is our love of Jesus. ~ Mother Teresa

Day 117: Do not say, "I'll pay you back for this wrong!" Wait for the Lord, and he will avenge you. ~ Proverbs 20:22

Day 118: God is an utterable sigh, planted in the depths of the soul. ~ Jean Paul

Day 119: Joy is a net of love by which you can catch souls. ~ Mother Teresa

Day 120: For through wisdom your days will be many, and years will be added to your life. ~ Proverbs 9:11

Day 121: God writes the Gospel not in the Bible alone, but also on trees, and in the flowers and clouds and stars. ~ Martin Luther

Day 122: A man can no more diminish God's glory by refusing to worship Him than a lunatic can put out the sun by scribbling the word darkness on the walls of his cell. ~ C.S. Lewis

Day 123: ~ Intense love does not measure, it just gives. ~ Mother Teresa

Day 124: The wise fear the Lord and shun evil, but a fool is hotheaded and yet feels secure. ~ Proverbs 14:16

Day 125: Freedom prospers when religion is vibrant and the rule of law under God is acknowledged. ~ Ronald Reagan

Day 126: I want you to be concerned for your next door neighbor. Do you know your next door neighbor? ~ Mother Teresa

Day 127: Gossips betray confidence, but the trustworthy keep a secret. ~ Proverbs 11:13

Day 128: If God would have wanted us to live in a permissive society He would have given us the ten suggestions and not the ten commandments. ~ Zig Ziglar

Day 129: The hunger for love is much more difficult to remove than the hunger for bread. ~ Mother Teresa

Day 130: One who has no sense shakes hands in pledge and puts up security for a neighbor. ~ Proverbs 17:18

Day 131: The Bible is one of the greatest blessings bestowed by God on the children of men. It has God for it's author; salvation for its end and truth without any mixture for its matter. It is all pure. ~ Johne Locke

Day 132: No harm overtakes the righteous, but the wicked have their fill of trouble. ~ Proverbs 12:21

Day 133: Love is a fruit in season at all times, and within reach of every hand. ~ Mother Teresa

Day 134: Choose my instruction instead of silver, knowledge rather than choice gold. ~ Proverbs 8:10

Day 135: A baby is God's opinion that life should go on. ~ Carl Sandburg

Day 136: Let us touch the dying, the poor, the lonely and the unwanted according to the graces we have received and let us not be ashamed or slow to do the humble work. ~ Mother Teresa

Day 137: Do not forsake wisdom, and she will protect you; love her and she will watch over you. ~ Proverbs 4:6

Day 138: Before God we are all equally wise—and equally foolish. ~ Albert Einstein

Day 139: If you can't feed a hundred people, then feed just one. ~ Mother Teresa

Day 140: Evildoers are trapped by their sinful talk, and so the innocent escape trouble. ~ Proverbs 12:13

Day 141: Read the Bible. Work hard and honestly. And don't complain. ~ Billy Graham

Day 142: Faith activates God—Fear activates the enemy. ~ Joel Osteen

Day 143: Being unwanted, unloved, uncared for, forgotten by everybody, I think that is a much greater hunger, a much greater poverty than the person who has nothing to eat. ~ Mother Teresa

Day 144: An inheritance claimed too soon will not be blessed at the end. ~ Proverbs 20:21

Day 145: Blessed are those who persevere under trial, because when they have stood the test, they will receive the crown of life that God has promised to those who love him. ~ James 1:12

Day 146: Spread love everywhere you go. Let no one ever come to you without leaving happier. ~ Mother Teresa

Day 147: The mouth of the righteous is a fountain of life, but the mouth of the wicked conceals violence. ~ Proverbs 10:11

Day 148: Before the throne of the Almighty, man will be judged not by his acts but by his intentions. For God alone reads our hearts. ~ Mahatma Ghandi

Day 149: We need to find God, and he cannot be found noise and restlessness. God is the friend of silence. See how nature—trees, flowers, grass—grows in silence; see the stars, the moon and the sun, how they move in silence…We need silence to be able to touch souls. ~ Mother Teresa

Day 150: Folly is bound up in the heart of a child, but the rod of discipline will drive it far away. ~ Proverbs 22:15

Day 151: Unless we form a habit of going to the Bible in bright moments as well as in trouble, we cannot fully respond to its consolations because we lack equilibrium between light and darkness. ~ Helen Keller

Day 152: When you focus on being a blessing, God makes sure that you are always blessed in abundance. ~ Joel Osteen

Day 153: Let us always meet each other with a smile, for the smile is the beginning of love. ~ Mother Teresa

Day 154: The teaching of the wise is a fountain of life, turning a person from the snares of death. ~ Proverbs 13:14

Day 155: God cannot give us happiness and peace apart from Himself, because it is not there. There is no such thing. ~ C.S. Lewis

Day 156: I have found the paradox, that if you love until it hurts, there can be no more hurt, only more love. ~ Mother Teresa

Day 157: Speak up for those who cannot speak for themselves, for the rights of all who are destitute. ~ Proverbs 31:8

Day 158: Question with boldness even the existence of a God; because, if there be one, he must more approve of the homage of reason, than that of blind-folded fear. ~ Thomas Jefferson

Day 159: Be faithful in small things, because it is in them your strength lies. ~ Mother Teresa

Day 160: Whoever loves discipline loves knowledge, but whoever hates correction is stupid. ~ Proverbs 12:1

Day 161: In all my perplexities and distresses, the Bible has never failed to give me light and strength. ~ Robert E. Lee

Day 162: Be strong and courageous. Do not be afraid or terrified because of them, for the Lord your God goes with you; he will never leave you nor forsake you. ~ Deuteronomy 31:6

Day 163: Let no one be found among you who sacrifices their son or daughter in the fire, who practices divination or sorcery, interprets omens, or engages in witchcraft. ~ Deuteronomy 18:10

Day 164: My son, pay attention to what I say; turn your ear to my words. ~ Proverbs 4:20

Day 165: Experience: that most brutal of teachers. But you learn. My God, do you learn. ~ C.S. Lewis

Day 166: Love the Lord your God with all your heart and with all your soul and with all your strength. ~ Deuteronomy 6:5

Day 167: Walk with the wise and become wise, for a companion of fools suffers harm. ~ Proverbs 13:20

Day 168: Mercy, peace and love be yours in abundance. ~ Jude 1:2

Day 169: Then Jesus declared, "I am the bread of life. Whoever comes to me will never go hungry, and whoever believes in me will never go thirsty." ~ John 6:35

Day 170: Righteousness exalts a nation, but sin condemns any people. ~ Proverbs 14:34

Day 171: The Bible is the rock on which the republic rests. ~ Andrew Jackson

Day 172: Let's swallow them alive, like the grave, and whole, like those who go down to the pit. ~ Proverbs 1:12

Day 173: Trust in the Lord and do good; dwell in the land and enjoy safe pasture. ~ Psalms 37:3

Day 174: Better a little with the fear of the Lord than great wealth with turmoil. ~ Proverbs 15:16

Day 175: The Lord helps them and delivers them; he delivers them from the wicked and saves them, because they take refuge in him. ~ Psalms 37:40

Day 176: Love is patient, love is kind. It does not envy, it does not boast, it is not proud. ~ 1 Corinthians 13:4

Day 177: A good name is more desirable than great riches; to be esteemed is better than silver or gold. ~ Proverbs 22:1

Day 178: Do not be deceived: God cannot be mocked. People reap what they sow. ~ Galatians 6:7

Day 179: Open my eyes that I may see wonderful things in your law. ~ Psalms 119:18

Day 180: In the Lord's hand the king's heart is a stream of water that he channels towards all who please him. ~ Proverbs 21:1

Day 181: The Bible is the cradle wherein Christ is laid. ~ Martin Luther

Day 182: Watch out for false prophets. They come to you in sheep's clothing, but inwardly they are ferocious wolves. ~ Mathews 7:15

Day 183: The unfolding of your words gives light; it gives understanding to the simple. ~ Psalms 119:130

Day 184: Many are the plans in a human heart, but it is the Lord's purpose that prevails. ~ Proverbs 19:21

Day 185: Turn, Lord, and deliver me; save me because of your unfailing love. ~ Psalms 6:4

Day 186: In him was life, and that life was the light of all people. ~ John 1:4

Day 187: The rich rule over the poor, and the borrower is slave to the lender. ~ Proverbs 22:7

Day 188: Then he said to them all: "Whoever wants to be my disciple must deny themselves and take their cross daily and follow me." ~ Luke 9:23

Day 189: Why do the wicked revile God? Why do they say to themselves, "He won't call us to account?"~ Psalms 10:13

Day 190: Blessed are those who find wisdom, those who gain understanding. ~ Proverbs 3:13

Day 191: The Bible tells us to love our neighbors; and also to love our enemies; probably because they are the same people. ~ Gilbert K. Chesterton

Day 192: Dear friends, let us love one another, for love comes from God. Everyone who loves has been born of God and knows God. ~ 1 John 4:7

Day 193: Not a word from their mouth can be trusted; their hearts are filled with malice. Their throat is an open grave; with their tongues they tell lies. ~ Psalms 5:9

Day 194: Those who have no sense deride their neighbors, but those who have understanding hold their tongues. ~ Proverbs 11:12

Day 195: Then Peter began to speak, "I now realize how true it is that God does not show favoritism." ~ Acts 10:34

Day 196: Do not cast me when I am old; do not forsake me when my strength is gone. ~ Psalms 71:9

Day 197: Wine is a mocker and beer a brawler; whoever is led astray by them is not wise. ~ Proverbs 20:1

Day 198: Above all, you must understand that no prophecy of scripture came about by the prophet's own interpretations of things. ~ 2 Peter 1:20

Day 199: The poor will eat and be satisfied; those who seek the Lord will praise him—may your hearts live forever! ~ Psalms 22:26

Day 200: Listen, my son, to your father's instruction, and do not forsake your mother's teaching. ~ Proverbs 1:8

Day 201: Put your nose in the Bible every day. It is your spiritual food. And then share it. Make a vow not to be a lukewarm Christian. ~ Kirk Cameron

Day 202: Go to the ant, you sluggard; consider its ways and be wise! ~ Proverbs 6:6

Day 203: For he has not despised or scorned the suffering of the afflicted one; he has not hidden his face from him, but has listened to his cry for help.~ Psalms 22:24

Day 204: The tongue has the power of life and death, and those who love it will eat its fruit. ~ Proverbs 18:21

Day 205: For I have kept the ways of the Lord; I am not guilty of turning from my God. ~ Psalms 18:21

Day 206: All whom the Father gives me will come to me, and whoever comes to me I will never drive away. ~ John 6:37

Day 207: The Lord brought me forth as the first of his works, before his deeds of old. ~ Proverbs 8:22

Day 208: The wicked say to themselves, "God will never notice; he covers his face and never sees." ~ Psalms 10:11

Day 209: Peace I leave with you; my peace I give you. I do not give to you as the world gives. Do not let your heart be troubled and do not be afraid. ~ John 14:27

Day 210: My son, if you accept my words and store up my commands within you. Proverbs 2:1

Day 211: I think Bible principles are principles for life. ~ Joel Osteen

Day 212: ~ In all your ways submit to him, and he will make your paths straight. Proverbs 3:6

Day 213: I lie down and sleep; I wake again because the Lord sustains me. ~ Psalms 3:5

Day 214: You are the salt of the earth. But if the salt loses its saltiness, how can it be made salty again? It is no longer good for anything, except to be thrown out and trampled underfoot. ~ Mathew 5:13

Day 215: The beginning of wisdom is this: Get wisdom. If it costs all you have, get understanding. ~ Proverbs 4:7

Day 216: I call out to the Lord, and he answers me from his holy mountain. ~ Psalms 3:4

Day 217: Get wisdom, get understanding; do not forget my words or turn away from them. ~ Proverbs 4:5

Day 218: In the past God overlooked such ignorance, but now he commands all people everywhere to repent. ~ Acts 17:30

Day 219: You who fear the Lord, praise Him! All you descendants of Jacob, honor him. Revere him, all you descendants of Israel. ~ Psalms 22:23

Day 220: My son, do not forget my teaching, but keep my commands in your heart. ~ Proverbs 3:1

Day 221: Hold fast to the Bible. To the influence of this book we are indebted to all the progress made in true civilization and to this we must look as our guide in the future. ~ Ulysses S. Grant

Day 222: Since, then, you have been raised with Christ, set your heart on things above, where Christ is seated at the right hand of God. ~ Colossians 3:1

Day 223: They are like a tree planted by streams of water, which yields its fruit in season and whose leaf does not wither—whatever they do prospers. ~ Psalms 1:3

Day 224: ~ Charm is deceptive, and beauty is fleeting; but a woman who fears the Lord is to be praised. ~ Proverbs 31:30

Day 225: For in him all things were created: things in heaven and on earth, visible and invisible, whether throne or powers or rulers or authorities; all things have been created through him and for him. ~ Colossians 1:16

Day 226: I keep my eyes always on the Lord. With him at my right hand, I will not be shaken. ~ Psalms 16:8

Day 227: To the discerning all of them are right; they are upright to those who have found knowledge. ~ Proverbs 8:9

Day 228: If I had cherished sin in my heart, the Lord would not have listened. ~ Psalms 66:18

Day 229: My sheep listen to my voice; I know them, and they follow me. ~ John 10:27

Day 230: The highway of the upright avoids evil; those who guard their ways preserve their lives. ~ Proverbs 16:17

Day 231: I try to speak in everyday language. I feel like God has gifted e to take Bible principles and make them practical. ~ Joel Osteen

Day 232: Honor the Lord with your wealth, with the first fruits of all your crops. ~ Proverbs 3:9

Day 233: For this reason a man will leave his father and mother and be untied with his wife, and they will become one flesh. ~ Genesis 2:24

Day 234: Give thanks to the Lord, for he is good; his love endures forever. ~ Psalms 107:1

Day 235: A friend loves at all times, and a brother is born for a time of adversity. ~ Proverbs 17:17

Day 236: Do not merely listen to the word, and so deceive yourselves. Do what it says. ~ James 1:22

Day 237: For the Lord watches over the way of the righteous, but the way of the wicked will be destroyed. ~ Psalms 1:6

Day 238: Those who conceal their sins do not prosper, but those who confess and renounce them find mercy. ~ Proverbs 28:13

Day 239: So I say, walk by the Spirit, and you will not gratify the desires of the sinful nature. ~ Galatians 5:16

Day 240: The Lord is close to the brokenhearted and saves those who are crushed in spirit. ~ Psalms 34:18

Day 241: The Bible will keep you from sin, or sin will keep you from the Bible. ~ Dwight L. Moody

Day 242: Commit to the Lord whatever you do and he will establish your plans. ~ Proverbs 16:3

Day 243: But if we walk in the light, as he is in the light, we have fellowship with one another, and the blood of Jesus, his Son, purifies us from all sin. ~ 1 John 1:7

Day 244: The Lord is my rock, my fortress and my deliverer, my God is my rock, in whom I take refuge, my shield and the horn of my salvation, my stronghold. ~ Psalms 18:2

Day 245: In their hearts human beings plan their course, but the Lord establishes their steps. ~ Proverbs 16:9

Day 246: Cast your cares on the Lord and he will sustain you; he will never let the righteous be shaken. ~Psalms 55:22

Day 247: Greater love has no one than this: to lay down one's life for one's friends. ~ John 15:13

Day 248: Pride goes before destruction, a haughty spirit before a fall. ~ Proverbs 16:18

Day 249: In you, Lord, I have taken refuge; let me never be put to shame. ~ Psalms 71:1

Day 250: A gentle answer turns away wrath, but a harsh word stirs up anger. ~ Proverbs 15:1

Day 251: I believe the Bible is the word of God from cover to cover. ~ Billy Sunday

Day 252: Not so the wicked! They are like the chaff that the wind blows away. ~ Psalms 1:4

Day 253: But he was pierced for our transgressions, he was crushed for our iniquities: the punishment that brought us peace was on him, and by his wounds we are healed. ~Isaiah 53:5

Day 254: For giving prudence to those who are simple, knowledge and discretion to the young. Proverbs 1:4

Day 255: One thing I ask from the Lord, this only do I seek: that I may dwell in the house of the Lord all the days of my life, to gaze on the beauty of the Lord, and to seek him in his temple. ~ Psalms 27:4

Day 256: In him we have redemption through his blood, the forgiveness of sins, in accordance with the riches of God's grace. ~ Ephesians 1:7

Day 257: There are six things the Lord hates, seven that are detestable to him. ~ Proverbs 6:16

Day 258: I have told you these things so that in me you may have peace. In this world you may have trouble. But take heart! I have overcome the world. ~ John 16:33

Day 259: For he will command his angels concerning you to guard you in all your ways. ~ Psalms 91:11

Day 260: A cheerful heart is good medicine, but a crushed spirit dries up the bones. ~ Proverbs 17:22

Day 261: I know the Bible is inspired because it inspires me. ~ Dwight L. Moody

Day 262: Do not judge or you too will be judged. ~ Mathew 7:1

Day 263: Even though I walk through the darkest valley, I fear no evil, because you are with me; your rod and your staff, they comfort me. ~ Psalms 23:4

Day 264: The fear of the Lord is the beginning of wisdom, and the knowledge of the Holy One is understanding. ~ Proverbs 9:10

Day 265: But those who hope in the Lord will renew their strength. They will soar on wings like eagles; they will run and not grow weary, they will walk and not be faint. ~ Isaiah 40:31

Day 266: Create in me a pure heart, O God, and renew a steadfast spirit within me. ~ Psalms 51:10

Day 267: For receiving instruction in prudent behavior, doing what is right and just and fair. ~ Proverbs 1:3

Day 268: A Psalm of David. The Lord is my shepherd, I lack nothing. ~ Psalms 23:1

Day 269: God made him who had no sin to be sin for us, so that in him we may become the righteousness of God. ~ 2 Corinthians 5:21

Day 270: Every word of God is flawless; he is a shield to those who take refuge in him. ~ Proverbs 30:5

Day 271: We can never learn too much of His will towards us, too much of His messages, and His advice. The Bible is His word and its study gives at once the foundation for our faith and an inspiration to battle onward in the fight against the tempter. ~ John D. Rockefellar

Day 272: As iron sharpens iron, so one person sharpens another. ~ Proverbs 27:17

Day 273: Is anyone among you sick? Let them call the elders of the church to pray over them and anoint them with oil in the name of the Lord. ~ James 5:14

Day 274: Children are a heritage from the Lord, offspring a reward from Him. ~ Psalms 127:3

Day 275: Where there is no revelation, people cast off restraint; but blessed are those who heed wisdom's instruction. ~ Proverbs 29:18

Day 276: Take delight in the Lord and he will give you the desires of your heart. ~ Psalms 37:4

Day 277: Blessed are those who do not walk in the step with the wicked or stand in the way that sinners take or sit in the company of mockers. ~ Psalms 1:1

Day 278: For he is the kind of person who is always thinking about the cost. "Eat and drink," he says to you, but his heart is not with you. ~ Proverbs 23:7

Day 279: For our struggle is not against flesh and blood, but against the rulers, against the authorities, against the powers of this dark world and against the spiritual forces of evil in the heavenly realms. ~ Ephesians 6:12

Day 280: "This then is how you should pray: "Our Father in heaven, hallowed be your name." ~ Mathews 6:9

Day 281: After I set out to refute Christianity intellectually and couldn't, I came to the conclusion the Bible was true and Jesus Christ was God's son. ~ Josh McDowell

Day 282: Whoever believes in the Son has eternal life, but whoever rejects the Son will not see life, for God's wrath remains on them. ~ John 3:36

Day 283: Brothers and sisters, we do not want you to be uninformed about those who sleep in death, so that you do not grieve like the rest who have no hope. ~1 Thessalonians 4:13

Day 284: There is a way that appears to be right, but in the end it leads to death. ~ Proverbs 14:12

Day 285: Keep your lives free from the love of money and be content with what you have, because God has said, "Never will I leave you, never will I forsake you." ~ Hebrews 13:5

Day 286: The light shines in the darkness, and the darkness has not overcome it. ~ John 1:5

Day 287: A wife of noble character whom can find? She is worth far more than rubies. ~ Proverbs 31:10

Day 288: This is how the birth of Jesus the Messiah came about: His mother Mary was pledged to be married to Joseph, but before they came together, she was found to be pregnant through the Holy Spirit. ~ Mathew 1:18

Day 289: Praise be to God and Father of our Lord Jesus Christ, who has blessed us in the heavenly realms with every spiritual blessing in Christ. ~ Ephesians 1:3

Day 290: The fear of the Lord is the beginning of knowledge but fools despise wisdom and instruction. ~ Proverbs 1:7

Day 291: Choosing to be positive and having a grateful attitude is going to determine how you're going to live your life. ~Joel Osteen

Day 292: But you are a chosen people, a royal priesthood, a holy nation, God's special possession, that you may declare the praises of him who called you out of darkness into his wonderful light. ~ 1 Peter 2:9

Day 293: Above all else guard your heart, for everything you do flows from it. ~ Proverbs 4:23

Day 294: He came to Jesus at night and said, "Rabbi, we know that you are a teacher that has come from God. For no one could perform the signs you are doing if God were not with him. ~ John 3:2

Day 295: You are the light of the world. A city on a hill cannot be hidden. ~ Mathew 5:14

Day 296: On one occasion an expert in the law stood up to test Jesus. "Teacher," he asked, "what must I do to inherit eternal life?" ~ Luke 10:25

Day 297: Or do you not know that wrongdoers will not inherit the kingdom of God? Do not be deceived: Neither the sexually immoral, nor idolaters, nor adulterers, nor male prostitutes, nor practicing homosexuals. ~ 1 Corinthians 6:9

Day 298: God said to Moses, "I am who I am. This is what you are to say to the Israelites. I am has sent me to you."~ Exodus 3:14

Day 299: The wind blows wherever it pleases. You hear its sound but you cannot tell where it comes from or where it is going. So it is with everyone born of the Spirit. ~ John 3:8

Day 300: "I am the true vine and my Father is the gardener." ~ John 15:1

Day 301: God didn't make a mistake when he made you. You need to see yourself as God sees you. ~ Joel Osteen

Day 302: Then the Lord God formed a man from the dust of the ground and breathed into his nostrils the breath of life, and the man became a living being. ~ Genesis 2:7

Day 303: And God said, "Let there be light," and there was light. ~ Genesis 1:3

Day 304: When Jesus spoke again to the people, he said, "I am the light of the world. Whoever follows me will never walk in darkness but will have the light of life." ~ John 8:12

Day 305: The Lord said to Abram, "Go from your country, your people, and your father's household to the land I will show you." ~ Genesis 12:1

Day 306: Whoever believes in him is not condemned, but whoever does not believe stands condemned already because they have not believed in the name of God's one and only son. ~ John 3:18

Day 307: Not everyone who says to me, 'Lord, Lord,' will enter the kingdom of heaven, but only those who do the will of my Father who is in heaven. ~ Mathew 7:21

Day 308: But in your hearts revere Christ as Lord. Always be prepared to give an answer to everyone who asks you to give the reason for the hope that you have. But do this with gentleness and respect. ~ 1 Peter 3:15

Day 309: I and the Father are one. ~ John 10:30

Day 310: To the Jews who had believed him, Jesus said, "If you hold my teaching, you really are my disciples." ~ John 8:31

Day 311: Do all you can to make your dreams come true. ~ Joel Osteen

Day 312: That you may know the certainty of things you have been taught. ~ Luke 1:4

Day 313: There was a rich man who was dressed in purple and fine linen and lived in luxury every day. ~ Luke 16:19

Day 314: Now this is eternal life: that they know you, the only true God, and Jesus Christ, whom you have sent. ~ John 17:3

Day 315: Because of the truth, which lives in us and will be with us forever. ~ 2 John 1:2

Day 316: In the past God spoke to our ancestors through the prophets at various times and in various ways. ~ Hebrews 1:1

Day 317: If any of you lacks wisdom, you should ask God, who gives you generously to all without finding fault, and it will be given to you. ~ James 1:15

Day 318: All of them were filled with the Holy Spirit and began to speak in other tongues as the Spirit enabled them. ~ Acts 2:4

Day 319: I am the vine: you are the branches. If you remain in me and I in you; you will bear much fruit; apart from me you can do nothing. ~ John 15:5

Day 320: Those who accepted his message were baptized, and about three thousand were added to their number that day. ~ Acts 2:41

Day 321: You can change your world by changing your words…Remember, death and life are in the power of the tongue. ~ Joel Osteen

Day 322: Start children off on the way they should go, and even when they are old they will not turn from it. ~ Proverbs 22:6

Day 323: Now the serpent was more crafty than any of the animals the Lord God had made. He said to the woman, "Did God really say, 'You must not eat from any tree in the graden?'" ~ Genesis 3:1

Day 324: Jesus said to her, "I am the resurrection and the life. Anyone who believes in me will live, even though they die." ~ John 11:25

Day 325: They replied, "Believe in the Lord Jesus, and you will be saved—you and your household." ~ Acts 16:31

Day 326: On the first day of the week we came together to break bread. Paul spoke to the people and, because he intended to leave the next day, he kept talking until midnight. ~ Acts 20:7

Day 327: Finally, brothers and sisters, whatever is noble, whatever is noble, whatever is right, whatever is pure, whatever is lovely, whatever is admirable—if anything is praiseworthy—think about such things. ~ Philippians 4:8

Day 328: After he said this, he was taken up before their very eyes, and a cloud hid him from their sight. ~ Acts 1:9

Day 329: When a Samaritan woman came to draw water, Jesus said to her, "Will you give me a drink?" ~ John 4:7

Day 330: He has shown all you people what is good. And what does the Lord require of you? To act justly and love mercy and to walk humbly with your God. ~ Micah 6:8

Day 331: God wants us to prosper financially, to have plenty of money, to fulfill His destiny laid out for us. ~ Joel Osteen

Day 332: The great dragon was hurled down—the ancient serpent called the devil, or Satan, who leads the whole world astray. He was hurled to the earth, and his angels with him. ~ Revelation 12:9

Day 333: Sanctify them by truth: your word is truth. ~ John 17:17

Day 334: While we wait for the blessed hope—the appearing of the glory, of our great God and Savior, Jesus Christ. ~ Titus 2:13

Day 335: Jesus replied, "Love the Lord your God with all your heart and with all your soul and with all your mind." ~ Mathew 22:37

Day 336: The son is the image of the invisible God, the firstborn over all creation. ~ Colossians 1:15

Day 337: Consider it pure joy, my brothers and sisters, whenever you face trials of many kinds. ~ James 1:2

Day 338: Then God said, "Let the land produce vegetation: seed bearing plants and trees on the land that bear fruit and produce seeds in it, according to their various kinds." And it was so. ~ Genesis 1:11

Day 339: "Then I saw a new heaven and a new earth," for the first heaven and the first earth had passed away, and there was no longer any sea. ~ Revelation 21:1

Day 340: Here I am! I stand at the door and knock. If anyone hears my voice and opens the door, I will come in and eat with them, and they with me. ~ Revelation 3:20

Day 341: Only God can look at somebody's heart. ~ Joel Osteen

Day 342: But the Advocate, the Holy Spirit, whom the Father will send in my name, will teach you all things and will remind you of everything I have said to you. ~ John 14:26

Day 343: As it is written: "There is no one righteous, not even one." ~ Romans 3:10

Day 344: So he made a whip out of cords, and drove all from the temple courts, both sheep and cattle; he scattered the coins of the money changers and overturned their tables. ~ John 2:15

Day 345: Let everyone be subject to the governing authorities, for there is no authority except that which God has established. The authorities which exist have been established by God. ~ Romans 13:1

Day 346: Finally be strong in the Lord and in his mighty power. ~ Ephesians 6:10

Day 347: The Spirit of the Lord is on me, because he has anointed me to proclaim the good news to the poor. He has sent me to proclaim freedom for the prisoners and recovery for sight of the blind, to set the oppressed free. ~ Luke 4:8

Day 348: But when he, the Spirit of truth comes, he will guide you into all the truth. He will not speak on his own; he will speak only what he hears, and he will tell you what is yet to come. ~John 16:13

Day 349: Keep watch over yourselves and all the flock of which the Holy Spirit has made you overseers. Be shepherds of the church of God, which he bought with his own blood.~ Acts 20:28

Day 350: For the grace of God has appeared that offers salvation to all people. ~ Titus 2:11

Day 351: You can be happy where you are. ~Joel Osteen

Day 352: You belong to your father, the devil and you want to carry out your father's desires. He was a murderer from the beginning, not holding to the truth, for there is no truth in him. When he lies, he speaks his native language for he is a liar and the father of lies. ~ John 8:44

Day 353: But seek first his kingdom and his righteousness, and all these things will be given to you as well. ~ Mathew 6:33

Day 354: Consequently, faith comes from hearing the message, and the message is heard through the word about Christ. ~ Romans 10:17

Day 355: Do not think that I have come to abolish the Law or the Prophets; I have not come to abolish them but to fulfill them. ~ Mathew 5:17

Day 356: When the Son of Man comes in all his glory, and all the angels with him, he will sit on his glorious throne. ~ Mathews 25:31

Day 357: And we know that in all things God works for the good of those who love Him, who have been called according to His purpose. ~ Romans 8:28

Day 358: Prospering just doesn't have to do with money. ~ Joel Osteen

Day 359: Jesus replied, "Very truly I tell you, no one can see the kingdom of God without being born again." ~ John 3:3

Day 360: The true light that gives light to everyone was coming into the world. ~ John 1:9

Day 361: Keep a good attitude and do the right thing even when it's hard. When you do that you are passing the test. And God promises your marked moments are on their way. ~ Joel Osteen

Day 362: Yet to all who did receive him, to those who believed in his name, he gave the right to become children of God. ~ John 1:12

Day 363: Peter replied, "Repent and be baptized, every one of you, in the name of Jesus Christ for the forgiveness of your sins. And you will receive the gift of the Holy Spirit. ~ Acts 2:38

Day 364: Then God said, "Let us make human beings in our image, in our likeness, so that they may rule over the fish in the sea and the birds in the sky, over the livestock and all the wild animals, and over all the animals that move along the ground. ~ Genesis 1:26

Day 365: For God so loved the world that he gave his one and only Son, that whosoever believeth in him shall not perish but have everlasting life. ~ John 3:16

22993489R00028

Printed in Poland
by Amazon Fulfillment
Poland Sp. z o.o., Wrocław